My Bible Activity Book

p

This is a Parragon Publishing Book
This edition published in 2004
Copyright © Parragon 2003
All rights reserved
Printed in Malaysia

Noah's Ark

Noah's Ark answers are on page 204-205

NOAH, A GOOD MAN

A long time ago, there was a man called Noah. Noah and his family were honest and kind. They worked hard and obeyed God.

But the world was filled with wicked people. God was angry that they disobeyed Him. He decided that the only way to end it would be to destroy the world and start again. But He wanted to save Noah and his family.

 Find the stickers to finish the picture.

Someone has hidden all these things.
Can you find them in the picture?
6 oranges   5 apples   4 bananas

NOAH BUILDS THE ARK

God spoke to Noah, and told him He was going to send a flood to destroy the world.

"You must build a big boat called an Ark, which will keep you safe," He said. God told Noah to make the Ark big enough to hold him and his family, along with two of every kind of animal.

Noah and his three sons, Ham, Shem and Japheth, built the Ark just as God told them to.

Find the stickers to finish the picture.

 Join the dots to finish the Ark. Now color it in. Can you find the stickers of Noah's three sons?

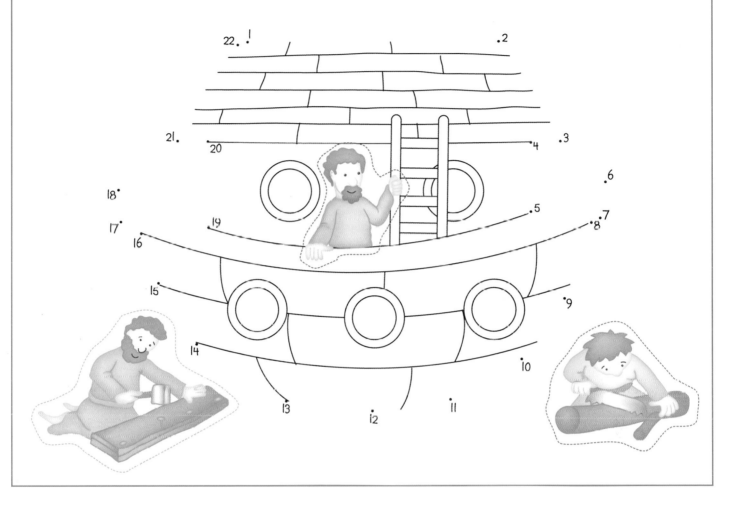

 Can you find all these words in the wordsearch?

Noah

Shem

Ham

Japheth

H	A	S	G	O	D	B	A	A
T	W	A	F	L	O	S	N	N
E	I	N	N	O	A	H	I	N
H	A	A	R	K	V	E	M	I
P	V	M	H	J	M	M	A	O
A	F	F	L	O	O	D	L	P
J	C	B	C	H	A	M	S	M

Flood

Ark

God

Animals

7

ALL ABOARD!

At last the Ark was ready! Noah gathered two of every kind of animal on Earth and led them on to the Ark.

There were animals that walked and trotted and ran, animals that crept and crawled and hopped, birds that flew and snakes that slithered.

All of them climbed aboard the Ark, where they would be safe from the flood.

Can you find the sticker of the monkeys?
Help them find the right path to the Ark.
Now find the stickers to make up the animal pairs.

1
2
3

THE RAIN COMES DOWN

Finally everyone was aboard the Ark. Then the rain began.

It rained and rained, for forty days and forty nights. Trees, houses, mountains and rivers all disappeared as the floodwater rose. The Earth was covered in water.

But the Ark sailed over the water, and everyone inside was safe and dry.

Find the stickers to feed the animals. There are six things that don't belong in the Ark. Can you find them all?

WATER, WATER, EVERYWHERE!

Finally the rain stopped, but the Ark kept sailing.

Noah looked out of the Ark. All he could see was water on every side. "But perhaps there is dry land somewhere," he thought.

Noah sent out a raven to look for dry land. It flew for miles and miles, but it found nowhere to land.

Then Noah sent out a dove. But the dove couldn't find anywhere to land, either, and soon came back to the Ark.

 Can you spot five differences between these two pictures?

Find the stickers to finish the picture.
Now color it in using the numbers below.

TIME TO LEAVE THE ARK

After a week Noah sent the dove out of the Ark again. This time it came back with an olive branch in its mouth.

"The dove found a tree peeking above the water," said Noah. "That means the floodwaters are going down."

When Noah sent the dove out again, it did not come back. It had found a dry place to nest. Noah looked out of the Ark and saw that the Earth was dry.

Find the stickers to complete the picture.

Help the dove find its way through the maze back to the Ark.

GOD'S PROMISE

Noah, his family and all the animals left the Ark. Noah thanked God for keeping the Ark safe in the flood. God promised that He would never again send a flood to destroy the Earth and its creatures.

"I have given you a sign of my promise," God told Noah. "Look up in the sky." Noah looked, and saw a beautiful rainbow above the clouds.

Now, whenever we see a rainbow after a storm, we remember God's promise, and know that He will always look after us.

 Find the stickers to finish the picture. Now color it in.

Pages 4/5

Page 6

Page 7

Pages 8/9

HOW MANY MICE?

God told Noah to build a big boat called an Ark.

How many mice can you find in the picture? Now color it in.

JUST COLOURING

Noah filled the Ark with two of every kind of creature, from the very smallest to the very biggest.

 Colour in this picture of elephants on their way to the Ark. Who are they carrying?

MATCHING PUZZLE

Noah loaded the Ark with lots of food for all the animals.

 Draw a line between each animal and its favourite food.

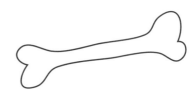

FIND TWO THE SAME

Noah gave each animal a special place to live on the Ark.

Can you find two pictures of Noah that are exactly the same?

a   b   c

d   e   f

MYSTERY PICTURE

When everything was ready, Noah shut the doors of the Ark and it started to rain.

 Carefully shade the dotted areas to discover a hidden picture.

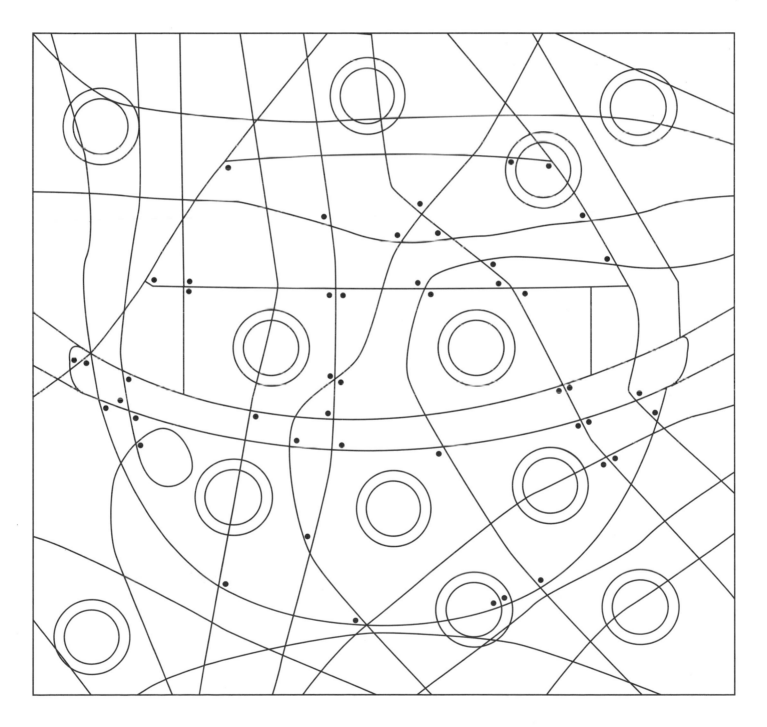

CROSSWORD

There were animals from every corner of the Earth on the Ark.

 Fill in the crossword using the pictures of animals as clues. Some letters have been added to help you.

4 down

1 down

2 across

5 across

6 across

3 down

MATCHING PUZZLE

Noah had to keep an eye on the naughty animals!

 Which shadow exactly matches the picture of this cheeky monkey?

AMAZING MAZE

Each animal had a mate to keep it company.

Can you help this Zebra find the way to its mate?

COPY THE PICTURE

Some of the tallest animals only just fitted in the Ark!

 Copy this picture of a giraffe, square by square, then color it in.

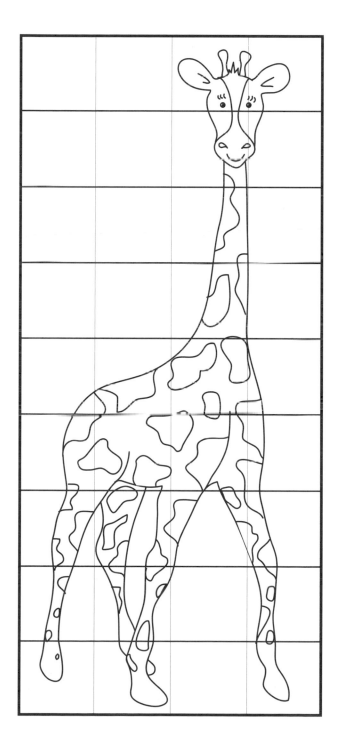

JUST COLOURING

Noah and his family fed all the animals every morning.

Colour in this picture.

EYE SPY

It rained for forty days and nights, but Noah and the animals were safe and warm inside the Ark.

Can you find five things beginning with the letter R in the picture? Now colour it in.

WHO'S MAKING ALL THAT NOISE?

Sometimes the noise inside the Ark was deafening!

Can you write in the noise each animal makes?

JUST COLOURING

When it stopped raining, Noah sent out a dove to look for dry land.

 Colour in the picture.

DOT TO DOT

On her second trip, the dove returned to the Ark with an olive branch in her beak. She had found dry land!

 Join the dots to find out who is carrying the olive branch. Now colour in the picture.

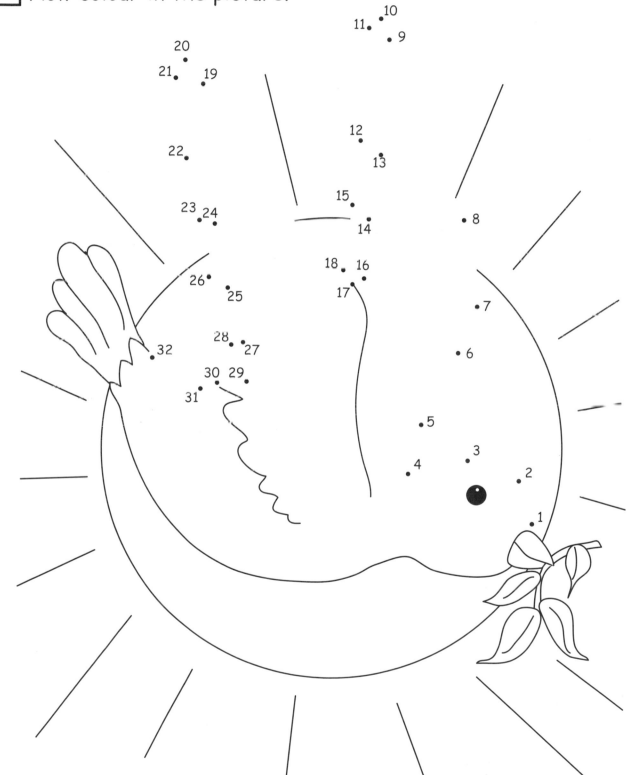

WORDSEARCH

Finally, it was time to leave the Ark! Out tumbled all the animals into the sunshine. God put a beautiful rainbow in the sky, as a sign of His love for the world.

Can you find these words in the grid?

CROCODILE   FROG
GIRAFFE   LIZARD
HORSE   GOAT
MONKEY   TIGER
DOG   OWL

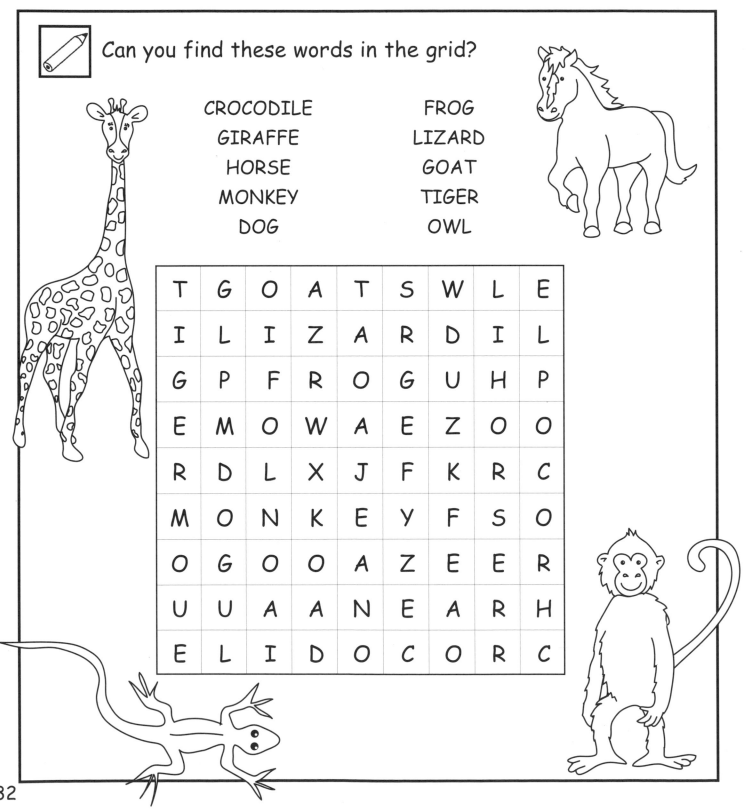

T	G	O	A	T	S	W	L	E
I	L	I	Z	A	R	D	I	L
G	P	F	R	O	G	U	H	P
E	M	O	W	A	E	Z	O	O
R	D	L	X	J	F	K	R	C
M	O	N	K	E	Y	F	S	O
O	G	O	O	A	Z	E	E	R
U	U	A	A	N	E	A	R	H
E	L	I	D	O	C	O	R	C

Jonah
and the
Whale

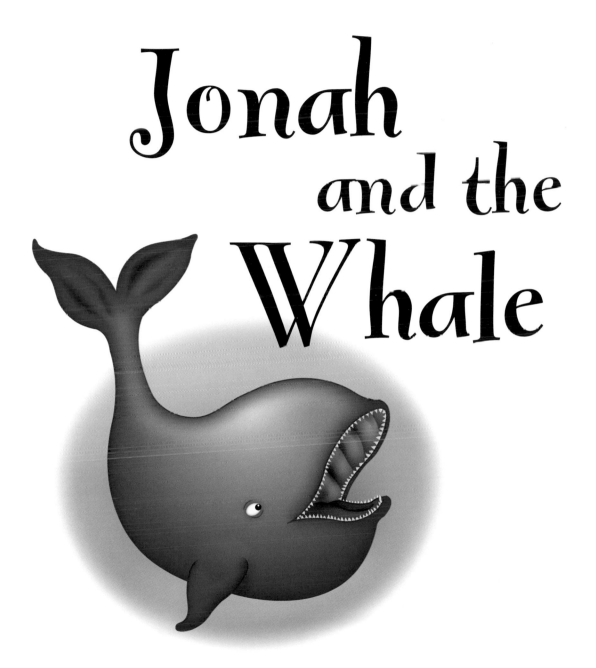

Jonah and the Whale answers are on page 206-207

One day, God spoke to a man named Jonah.

"Go to the city of Nineveh," God told Jonah. "The people there are very wicked. Go and tell them to change their ways and follow my laws."

But Jonah didn't like the people of Nineveh, and he didn't want to do what God asked him. So he found a boat that was sailing to a far away land.

Follow the ropes to help Jonah get on the right boat.
Find the stickers to finish the picture. Now color it in.

a
b
c

34

35

Jonah paid his fare and got on the boat. He went below deck and fell fast asleep.

When the boat sailed out of the harbor, a terrible storm blew up. The boat was flung back and forth over the waves. The sailors tried to row back towards shore, but the storm was too strong.

"Get rid of some of our cargo to make the boat lighter," said the captain. So the sailors tossed the cargo overboard.

Find the stickers to finish the picture.

Here are two pictures of Jonah asleep below deck. Can you spot ten differences between them?

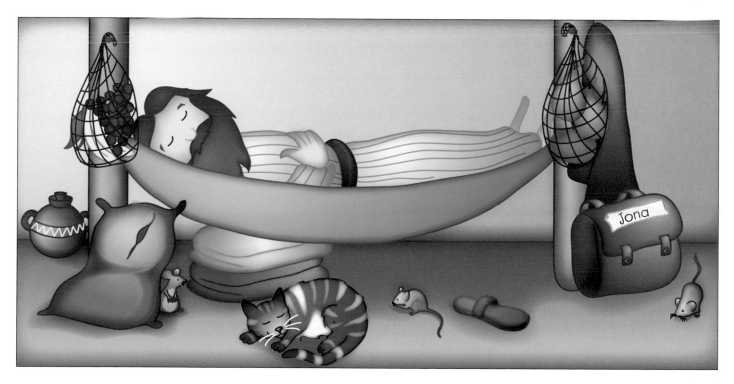

DRAWING LOTS

The storm grew worse, and the sailors were terrified.

"Help us!" they cried to their gods. But the storm raged on.

Then the captain said, "One of the gods must be angry with someone on the boat. Let's draw lots to find out who. Then we can throw him overboard."

So they wrote down everyone's name, and put the names in a sack. Then the captain picked out one name.

Find the stickers to finish the picture. Can you find six rats hidden in the scene?

Put all the sailors' names in the grid below.
Whose name is hidden down the middle?

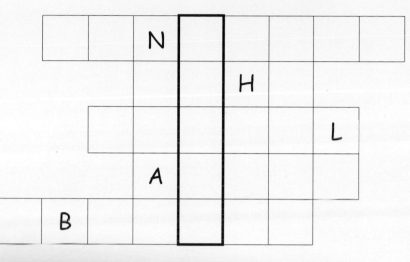

Just then, Jonah woke up. He came up on deck.

"The storm is my fault," he said. "My god is the one true God. He is angry with me, because I did not do what He asked. Throw me overboard, and the storm will end."

The sailors tossed him overboard. Suddenly, the storm was over!

"Jonah's god *is* the one true God!" cried the sailors. They fell to their knees and prayed, thanking God for ending the storm.

 Draw a line to match each of the fish below to its partner. Find the stickers to finish the picture, then color it in.

41

Jonah splashed into the waves, and sank down to the bottom of the sea. He knew he would drown unless God helped him.

God did help Jonah. As he came up again, a huge sperm whale came along and swallowed him.

It was very dark inside the whale's belly, and Jonah was frightened. But he knew that God can see even into the farthest, darkest places, and so he prayed to God to save him.

Find the stickers to complete the picture. Now join the dots.

Here are two pictures of Jonah in the whale's belly. Can you spot five differences between them?

 What has swallowed Jonah?
Unscramble the letters to find out.

E R M P S   H E W L A

_ _ _ _ _   _ _ _ _ _

43

Jonah was in the whale's belly for three days. But he never stopped believing that God would save him. And he was right.

On the third day, God made the whale spit Jonah on to dry land. Jonah was so happy that he said a prayer of thanks to God.

He promised that, from now on, he would do whatever God asked of him.

Find the stickers to complete the picture.

What do the signs say? Use the code below to find out.

God spoke to Jonah again, and told him to go to the city of Nineveh. This time Jonah went. He told the people to give up their wicked ways and obey the word of God.

The people of Nineveh listened to Jonah, and promised to change their ways.

And, just as He had forgiven Jonah, God forgave the people of Nineveh.

 Help Jonah find his way to the temple. Find the stickers to finish both pictures.

Color the picture.

47

There are eight differences between these two pictures. Can you find them all?

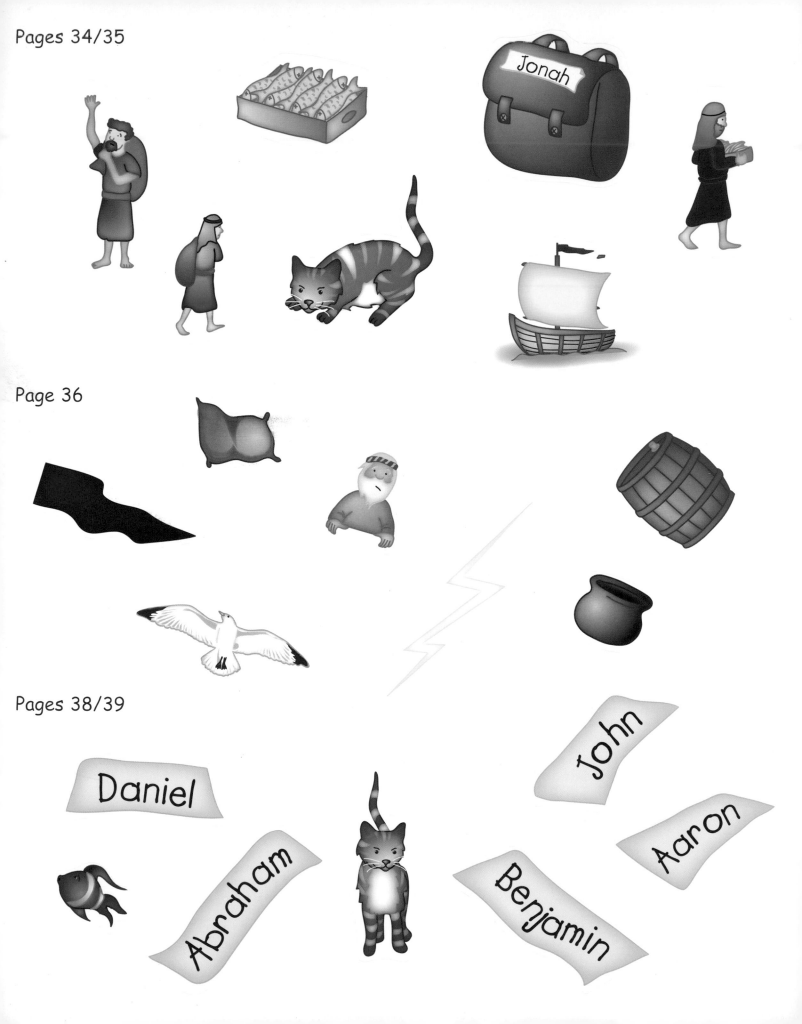

Pages 34/35

Page 36

Pages 38/39

Pages 40/41

Page 42

Pages 44/45

Pages 46/47

SPOT THE DIFFERENCE

God asked Jonah to go to Nineveh, but Jonah didn't want to go.

 Two of these pictures of Jonah are exactly the same.
Can you find them?

a

b

c

d

e

f

FINISH THE PICTURES

Instead, Jonah went to the harbor. He found a boat sailing to a distant land, far away from Nineveh.

 Can you make these four boats look exactly the same?

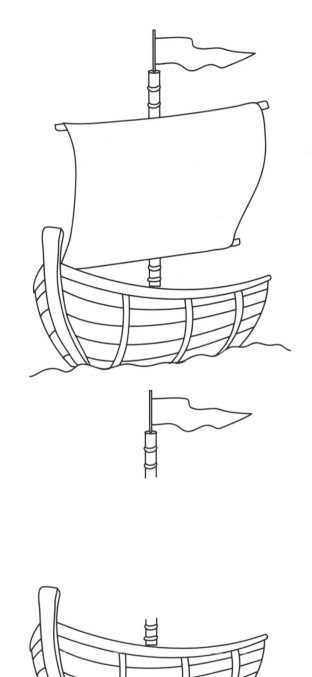

JUST COLORING

Jonah got on the boat, even though he knew he was disobeying God.

Color in the picture.

FIND TWO THE SAME

The sailors on the boat had no idea what Jonah was up to.

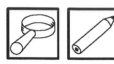 Only two of these sailors are exactly the same. Can you draw a line between them?

a
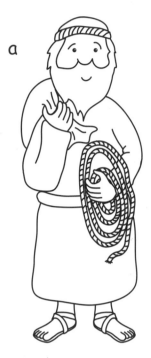

b
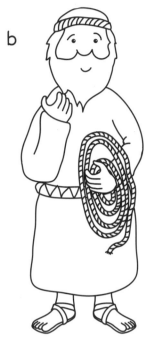

c

d

e

f
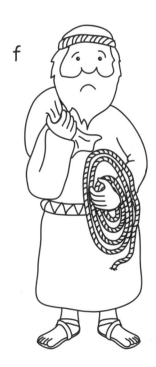

MATCHING GAME

The boat set off for the distant land, with Jonah on board.

 Can you match each picture with its shadow?

EYE SPY

Jonah felt very relieved that he was not going to Nineveh!

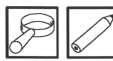 How many things beginning with the letter S can you find in this picture? Now color it in.

COPY THE PICTURE

After a while, Jonah went below deck and fell asleep.

 Copy this picture using the grid as a guide.

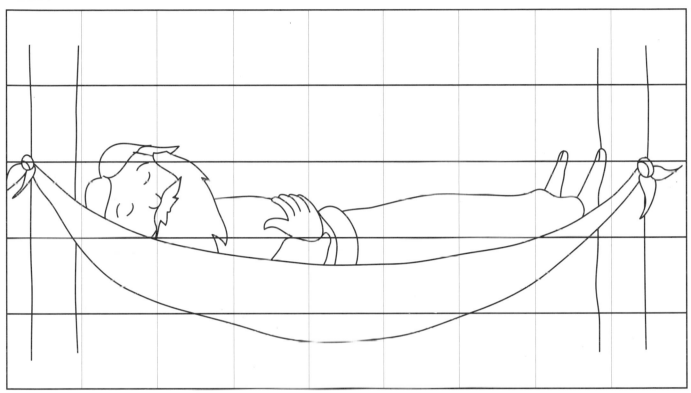

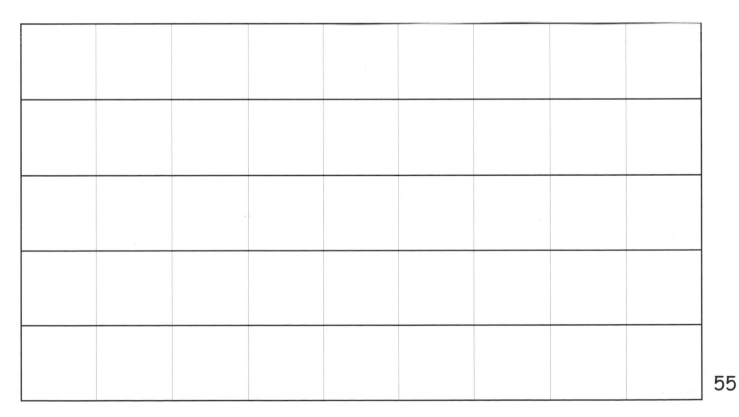

HOW MANY BOATS?

God was very angry with Jonah. He sent a storm that tossed the boat on the waves.

How many boats can you find in the big picture?

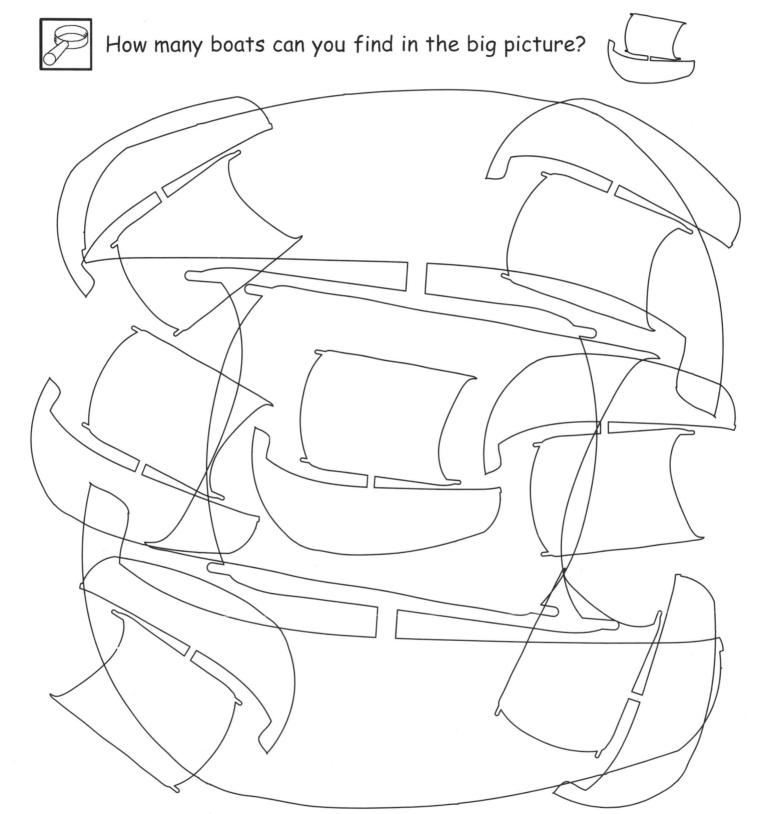

DOT TO DOT

Jonah told the sailors to throw him overboard.

Join the dots to finish the picture. Now color it in.

As soon as the sailors threw Jonah overboard, the storm stopped at once.

How many crabs can you find in the picture?

God sent an enormous whale to rescue Jonah.

 Shade the dotted areas to reveal the hidden picture.

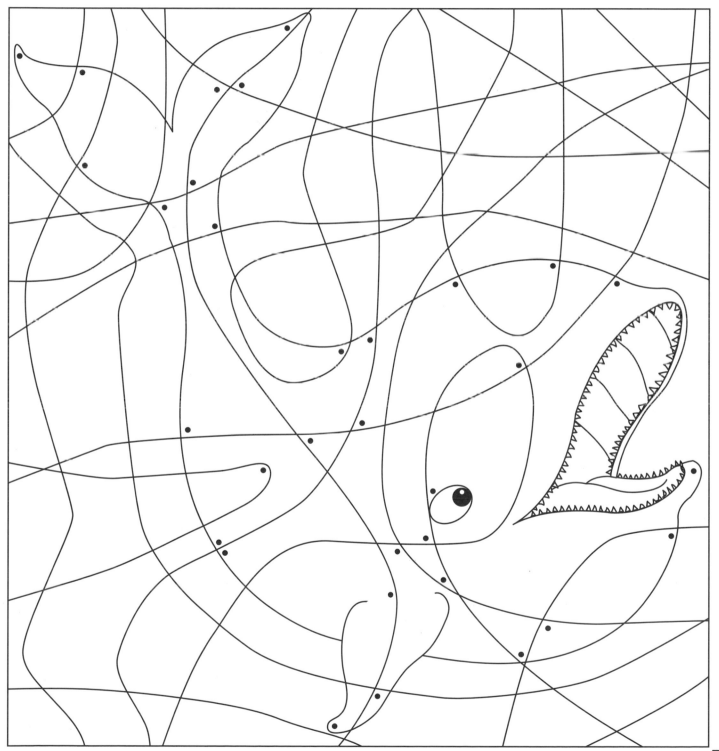

SPOT THE DIFFERENCE

The whale swallowed Jonah whole.

 Which picture is not the same as the others?

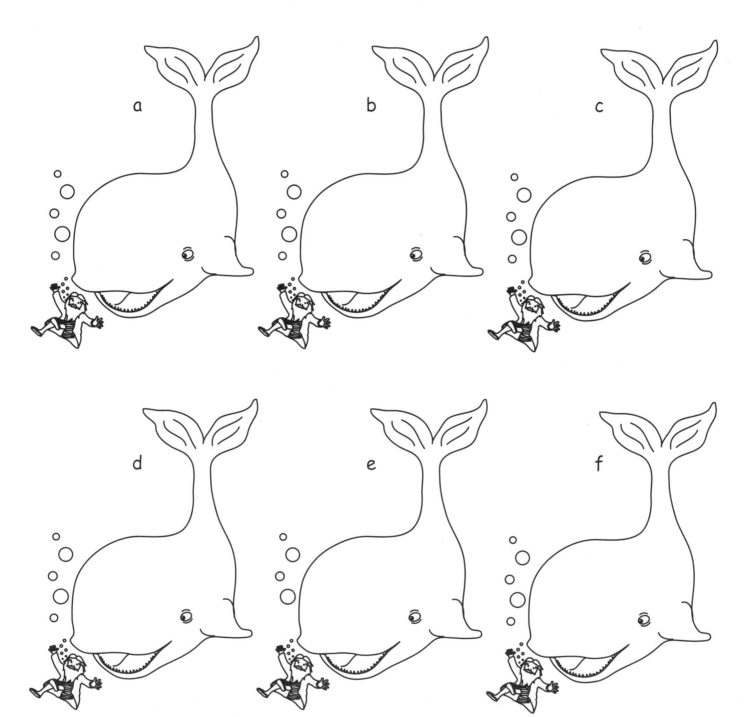

JIGSAW PUZZLE

Poor Jonah lived for three days in the whale's belly!

Color in the pieces needed to make up this picture of the whale.

EYE SPY

Inside the whale, Jonah prayed to God every day to save him.

 The whale has swallowed lots of other things, too! Which ones don't belong in the picture, because they are too modern?

WORDSEARCH

God did not forget about Jonah. He listened to his prayers.

Can you find these words in the grid?

BOAT   WHALE

BARREL   NINEVEH

STORM   FISH

SAILOR   SEA

B	O	A	T	C	G	F	V	N
A	S	E	A	N	U	L	I	N
R	O	P	E	U	D	N	V	E
R	W	B	A	S	E	R	E	O
E	H	H	P	V	O	O	L	F
L	A	E	E	L	H	J	Z	I
E	L	H	I	L	L	E	V	S
U	E	A	A	N	E	A	R	H
B	S	T	O	R	M	M	J	F

God made the whale spit Jonah out onto dry land. Jonah was so happy that he said a prayer of thanks. Then he set off for Nineveh to teach the people, just as God had asked.

Color in the picture.

Moses in the Bulrushes

Moses in the Bulrushes answers are on page 208-209

SLAVES IN EGYPT

The Israelites had lived happily in the land of Egypt for many, many years. But the King of Egypt, called Pharaoh, was worried.

He saw that the Israelites were growing in number, and he was afraid that they would try to take over his land.

So Pharaoh made the Israelites slaves and forced them to work for cruel Egyptian masters.

 Find the stickers to complete the picture.

A CRUEL LAW

Still the number of Israelites grew and grew, so Pharaoh made a cruel new law.

Pharaoh told his guards, "Every Israelite baby boy must be put to death!"

 Spot the 5 differences between the two pictures.

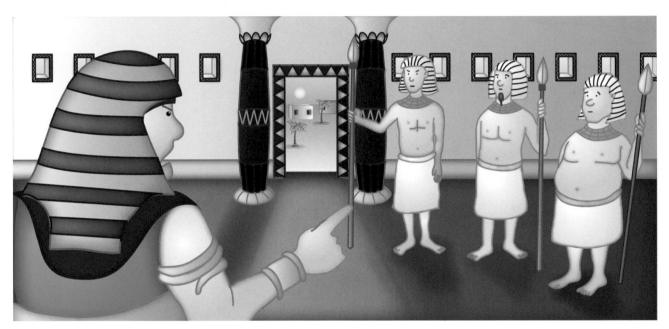

An Israelite woman named Yocheved had two children. Their names were Aaron and Miriam. When Yocheved heard about the law, she was very upset, because she was expecting a baby.

Find the stickers to complete the picture. Now color it in.

HIDING THE BABY

Yocheved had her baby, and the whole family rejoiced. But they knew they would have to keep the baby hidden because it was a boy.

Aaron and Miriam kept watch at the windows. If they saw Pharaoh's soldiers nearby, they warned their mother. Yocheved always managed to find a safe place to hide the baby.

 Fill up the hiding places with the right stickers. Where has Yocheved hidden her baby?

THE BABY IN THE BULRUSHES

When the baby was three months old, he got too big to hide. So Yocheved made a plan.

She went to the river and gathered some bulrushes to make a basket, just big enough to hold the baby. Then she put her baby inside, wrapped up in a warm blanket. She and Miriam took the basket to the river, and hid it among the reeds.

"Stay here and watch your baby brother," Yocheved told Miriam. "Come and tell me what happens to him."

How many frogs can you find in this picture?
Can you find two that are exactly the same as each other?
Now find the stickers to complete the picture.

PHARAOH'S DAUGHTER

Miriam hid in the tall grass near the river, and watched carefully.

In a little while, Pharaoh's daughter came down to the river to bathe.
Miriam was very worried – what would happen if the baby was found?

As the princess waded in to the river, she saw the basket in the reeds.
"What can that be?" the princess wondered.

 Find the stickers to finish the picture.
Who will reach the basket?

The princess looked inside the basket and saw a baby boy.

"This must be an Israelite baby!" she said. "He is so small and sweet – I won't let anyone harm him. I will take him back to the palace and raise him as my own."

When Miriam heard this, she had an idea. Coming out of her hiding place, she asked Pharaoh's daughter, "Shall I find an Israelite woman to be the baby's nurse?"

The princess said yes, and Miriam raced home to get her mother.

 Find five stickers to finish dressing the princess.

Find the right route to help
Miriam get home quickly.

MOSES THE PRINCE

Pharaoh's daughter named the baby Moses, which means "draw out", because she drew him out of the water. And he was raised by his mother, Yocheved in Pharaoh's palace.

Moses grew up as an Egyptian prince, but when he was old enough, his mother told him the story of his birth. So Moses knew that he was an Israelite, and that God had saved his life. When he was older, Moses became his people's greatest leader. He led the Israelites out of slavery in Egypt into the promised land of Israel.

 Find the stickers to complete the picture.
Now color in the scene of Pharaoh's palace.

There are eight differences between these two pictures. Can you find them all?

Pages 66/67

Page 69

Pages 70/71

Pages 72/73

Pages 74/75

Page 76

Pages 78/79

SPOT THE DIFFERENCE

The Pharaoh of Egypt made the Israelite people work as slaves for cruel Egyptian masters.

These pictures all look the same, but look more closely. Can you spot the one which is different?

a

b

c

d

e

f

EYE SPY

Then the Pharaoh made a new law. All Israelite baby boys must be killed!

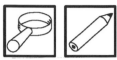 Can you find five things that don't belong in this picture? Now color it in.

WHICH WAY?

The Pharoah's guards visited every Israelite home to search for baby boys.

 Which path should the guards take to find their way to the Israelite house?

a

b

c

COPY THE PICTURE

One woman, called Yocheved, hid her son in a basket in the river, to save him.

 Copy this picture, square by square, then color it in.

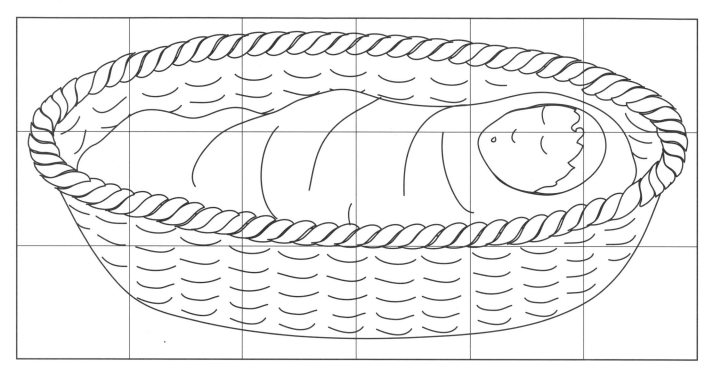

DOT TO DOT

The baby's sister, Miriam, hid in the bulrushes on the river bank, to watch over her little brother.

 Join the dots to show who is hiding in the bulrushes. Now color in the picture.

85

FIND TWO THE SAME

The Pharaoh's daughter came to the river to bathe with her servants.

Two of these servant girls are exactly the same. Can you draw a line between them?

a

b

c

d

e

f

HOW MANY?

The princess and her servants walked along the river bank, in the shade of the palm trees.

How many palm trees can you spot in the big picture?

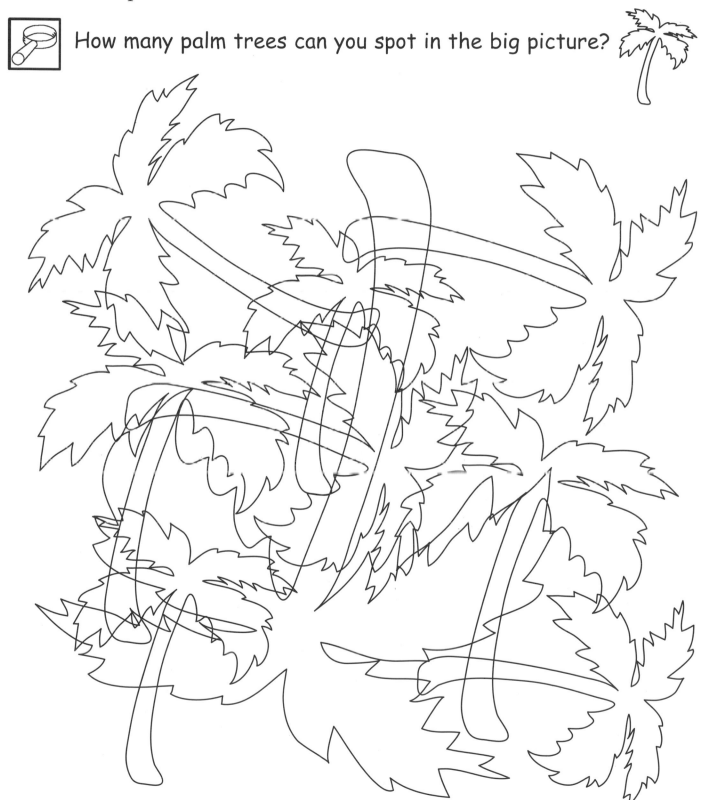

CROSSWORD

The princess waded into the river to bathe, right next to the basket.

Fill in the crossword using the pictures as clues. Some letters have been added to help you.

3 across

2 across

1 down

3 down

2 down

4 across

JUST COLORING

The princess and her servants couldn't believe their eyes when they found a baby among the bulrushes.

Color in this picture.

MATCHING PUZZLE

The princess decided to bring the baby up as her own son.

 Can you match the princess with the right shadow?

WORDSEARCH

Miriam offered to find an Israelite woman to be the baby's nurse. The princess agreed, so Miriam rushed home to fetch her mother.

Can you find these words in the grid below?

YOCHEVED   PHARAOH

PYRAMID   MOSES

BULRUSHES   MIRIAM

BASKET   POT

PRINCESS   FAN

S	P	M	I	R	P	N	M	J
E	Y	P	H	A	R	A	O	H
H	R	O	W	K	I	G	S	M
S	A	P	C	S	N	B	E	A
U	M	O	S	H	C	I	S	I
R	I	T	O	E	E	L	Q	R
L	D	N	A	F	S	V	U	I
U	X	F	O	P	S	H	E	M
B	A	S	K	E	T	S	D	D

COMPLETE THE PICTURE

The princess brought up the baby, Moses, in the palace, with the help of Yocheved.

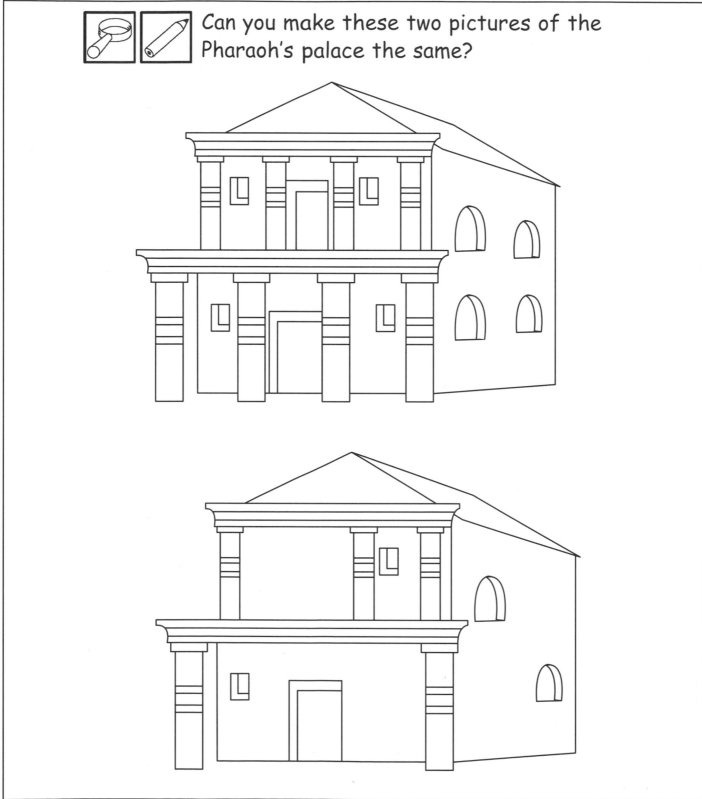

Can you make these two pictures of the Pharaoh's palace the same?

EYE SPY

Moses was treated like an Egyptian prince, even though he was an Israelite.

Can you find these five things in the picture?
Now color it in.

DOT TO DOT

Moses grew up a happy, strong boy at the palace.

 Join the dots to complete the picture. Now color it in.

COPY THE PICTURES

When he was old enough, the princess told Moses how she found him as a little Israelite baby.

Can you make these four pictures of the princess all look exactly the same?

JUST COLORING

Moses never forgot that he was an Israelite. One day he would become their greatest leader, and save his people from slavery.

 Color in this picture of Moses grown up.

David and Goliath

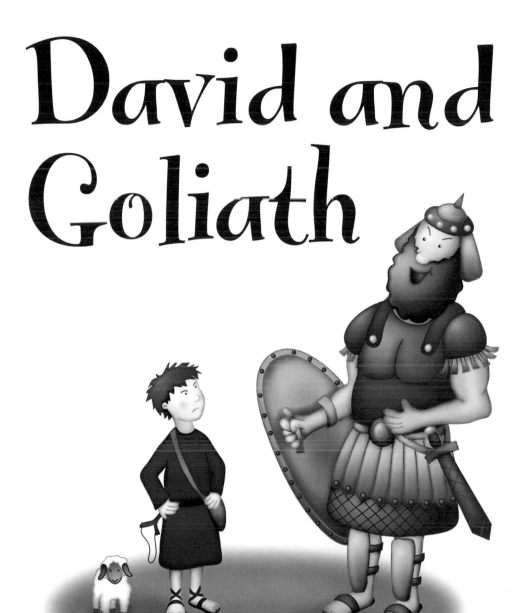

David and Goliath answers are on page 210-211

DAVID THE SHEPHERD

Long ago there was a boy called David. He spent most of his time guarding his father's sheep in the fields.

In the day David practised with his sling. When a lion or bear scared the sheep, David sent it off with a stone from his sling.

At night David played his harp and talked to God. He knew God was always there, protecting him as he protected the sheep.

 Find the stickers to complete the picture.
How many sheep can you spot in this picture?

DAVID SEES GOLIATH

One morning David's father asked him to take food to his brothers.

When David reached the soldiers' camp, all the Israelite soldiers were trembling with fear. David soon saw why they were so scared, for just then Goliath stepped forward.

"There is no one in your army brave enough to fight me!" shouted Goliath. "You are all cowards and we Philistines will conquer you all!"

Find the stickers to complete the picture. Which is the safest route for David to take to his brothers?

"How can you let him talk that way?" David asked his brothers.

"Look at him!" said David's brother Eliab. "He is too big and strong for anyone."

"I will fight him," said David. "I am not afraid."

His brothers just laughed at him.

But David told his brothers once again that he wanted to fight Goliath, so they took him to King Saul.

"You are so small," said the King. "How can you fight Goliath?"

"I have fought the lions and bears that attacked my father's sheep," said David. "I know I can fight Goliath. God will help me."

We have lots of things now which didn't exist in David's time. Can you spot the ten modern things in this pile of armor?

"If you must fight," said Saul, "then use my sword and wear my armor to protect you."

David put on the King's armor, but it was too big and heavy. So was the sword.

Find the stickers to dress David in King Saul's armor, and find the King's sword for him to hold.

FIVE SMOOTH STONES

David took off King Saul's armor and went down to the river. He chose five smooth stones for his sling and went to meet Goliath.

When Goliath saw him coming, he roared with laughter. "Is this what the Israelites send to fight me? A boy?"

"I may be a boy," replied David, "but God is with me."

 Can you spot five differences between these two pictures?

"Where are your weapons?" asked Goliath, holding up his sword and spear.

David was not afraid. "You may have a sword and a spear," he told Goliath, "but I have the strength of God. He will help me to defeat you!"

 Can you find the stickers of David and Goliath's weapons?

DAVID TAKES AIM

Goliath came towards David, his sword raised. David stepped forward to meet Goliath. He reached into his bag for one of the smooth stones, and put it in his slingshot. Then he took aim.

The stone went sailing through the air. Then…THWACK! It hit Goliath right in the middle of his forehead. With a mighty groan, the giant fell to the ground.

David had won!

Join the dots to see the picture of David and Goliath.

108

Can you find the story stickers and put them in order?
Read the scrolls to help you.

Picture 1

Goliath came towards David, his sword raised.

Picture 2

David reached into his bag for one of the smooth stones.

Picture 3

The stone went sailing through the air.

Picture 4

Goliath fell to the ground. David had won!

DAVID THE HERO

Cheering and shouting with joy, the Israelites crowded around David.

The Philistines, seeing that Goliath was dead, turned and ran away in fear. The Israelites had won the battle.

David became a great soldier, and he won many more battles. Years later, when King Saul died, David became King of Israel—one of the greatest kings of all time.

 Find the stickers to finish the picture.
Now color the scene.

SPOT THE DIFFERENCE

 Can you spot nine differences between these two pictures?

Pages 98/99

Pages 100

Pages 102/103

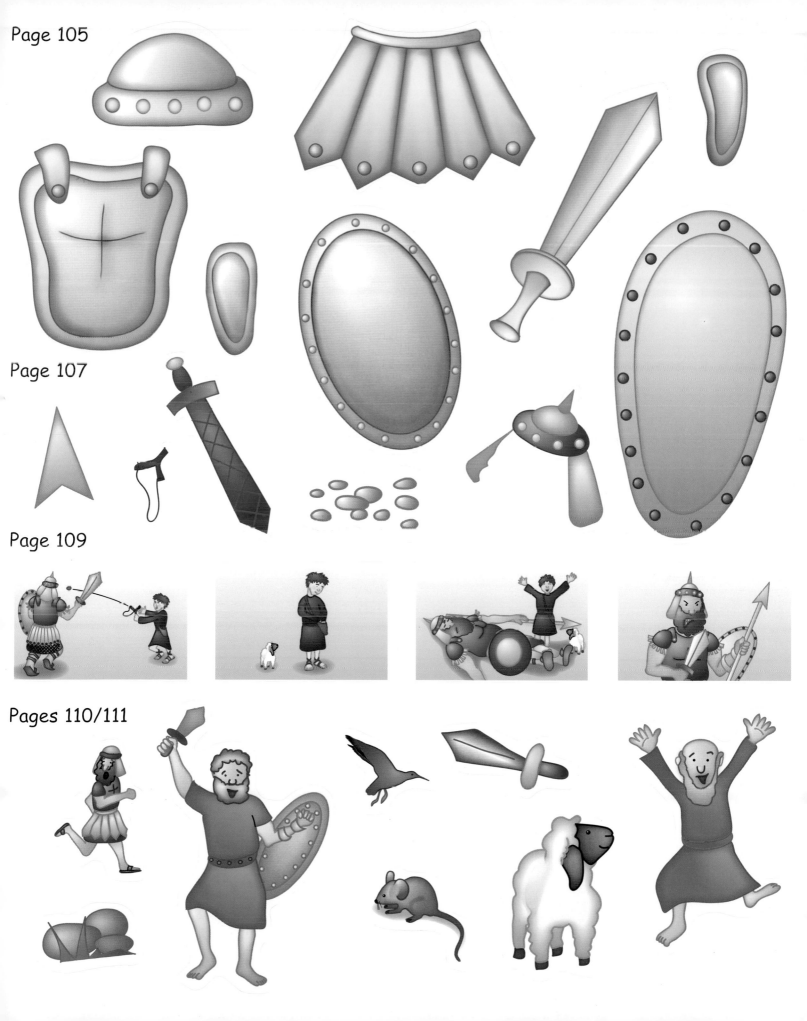

Page 105

Page 107

Page 109

Pages 110/111

COPY THE PICTURE

David was a young shepherd boy who trusted in God. He spent most of the time guarding his father's sheep in the fields.

 Can you copy this picture of David, using the grid as a guide?

MIX AND MATCH

David loved to play his harp and talk to God.

 This picture has been jumbled up. Can you work out what it is?

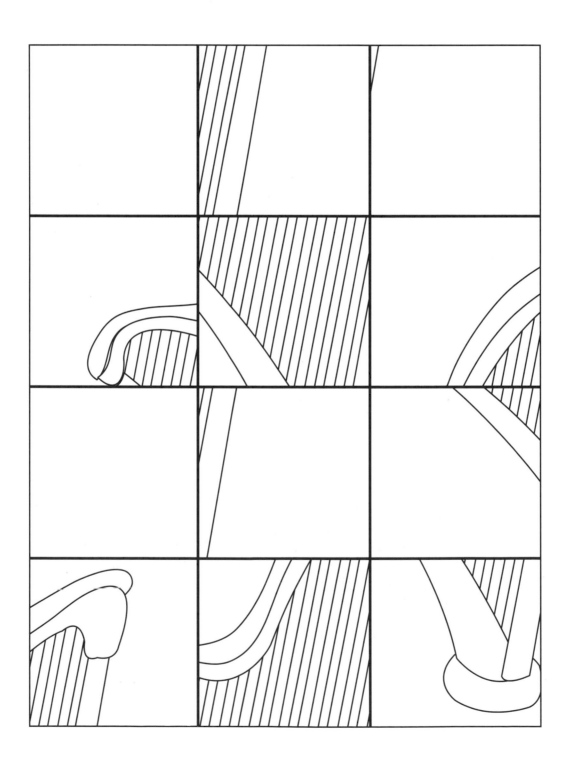

SPOT THE DIFFERENCE

Sometimes David even played his harp for the King, Saul.

These pictures of Saul look the same, but one is different. Can you draw a circle around it?

WHICH WAY?

David used a slingshot to protect his flock of sheep from wild animals.

 Which path should David take to find his slingshot?

DOT TO DOT

David was a good shot with his sling, because he used it every day.

 Join the dots to discover which animal David is chasing away. Now color in the picture.

FIND TWO THE SAME

David had seven brothers who were in the army, fighting the Philistines.

 Look closely. Can you find two Philistine soldiers dressed exactly the same?

MATCHING GAME

One day, David took food to his brothers. They were getting ready to fight the Philistine army.

 Follow the tangled string to help each person find the right weapon.

COPY THE PICTURE

The Philistine army had one soldier who was much bigger and stronger than all the others, called Goliath. No one wanted to fight with him.

 Copy this picture of Goliath, square by square, then color it in.

WORDSEARCH

David decided to fight Goliath himself. "With God's help, I can defeat him," he cried bravely.

Can you find these words in the grid?

ISRAELITE	GIANT
BEAR	GOAT
LION	SHEEP
GOLIATH	HARP
SAUL	DAVID

E	A	Z	S	D	I	V	A	D
B	T	G	A	E	G	I	L	D
E	A	I	U	E	O	E	I	P
A	O	A	L	B	L	I	O	N
L	G	N	T	E	I	R	T	O
H	I	T	Y	A	A	F	E	I
A	M	O	X	R	T	R	A	U
R	O	E	P	G	H	K	S	L
P	E	E	H	S	Q	H	T	I

MATCHING GAME

King Saul offered to lend David his armor, but it was much too big and heavy for him.

Can you draw a circle around the shadow that exactly matches this picture of David?

a

b

c

d

e

AMAZING MAZE

"I don't need armor!" said David. "God will protect me."

Help David find his way across the battlefield to Goliath.

EYE SPY

David put a small smooth pebble in his slingshot and turned to face Goliath.

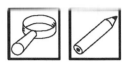 How many things beginning with the letter S can you spot in the picture? Now color it in.

HOW MANY?

Goliath raised his sword, laughing, ready to fight.

How many swords can you see in the big picture?

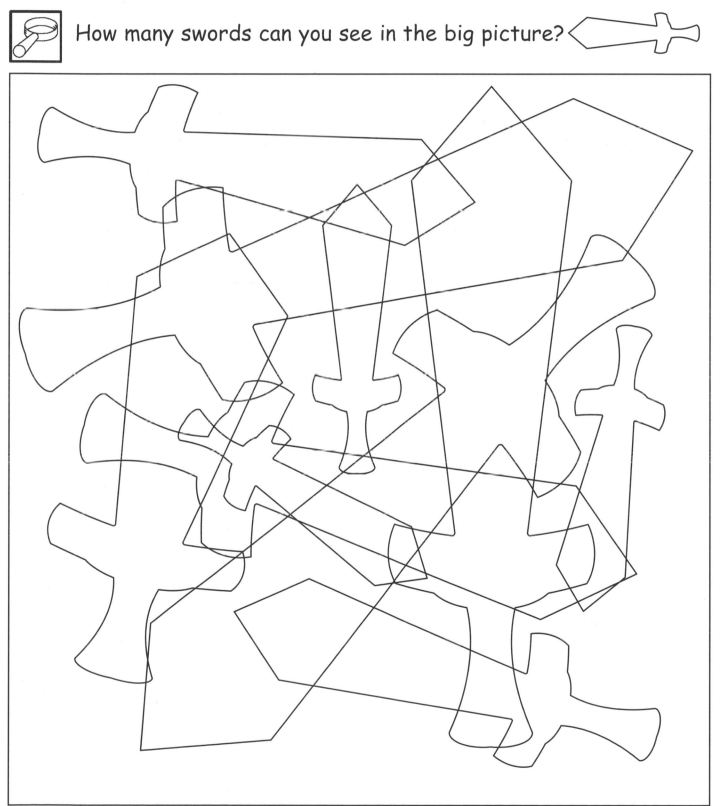

CROSSWORD

David took careful aim with his sling. PING! The pebble shot through the air.

Fill in the crossword using the pictures as clues. Some letters have been added to help you.

2 across

3 down

1 down

¹S

²S   L

³S   I   G

R   R

D

2 down

3 across

SPOT THE DIFFERENCE

The pebble struck Goliath on the forehead, and he fell to the ground.

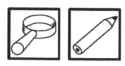 There are nine differences between these two pictures. How many can you spot?

JUST COLORING

Many years later David became King of Israel—one of the greatest kings of all time.

Color this picture of King David.

Joseph's Coat of Many Colors

Joseph's Coat of Many Colors answers are on page 212-213

Long ago, in a land called Canaan, there lived a boy called Joseph. Joseph's father, Jacob, had many goats and many sons to look after them.

Jacob loved all his sons, but he loved Joseph best of all. Jacob gave Joseph a coat of many different colors. But this made Joseph's brothers angry and jealous.

Find the stickers of Joseph's eleven brothers to complete the picture.

Simeon

Judah

Reuben

Issachar

Gad

Dan

Asher

Levi

Benjamin

Zebulun

Naphtali

Using the numbers below, color in Joseph's colorful coat.

One night, Joseph had a strange dream. The next day, he told his brothers about it.

"I dreamt that we were out in the fields, tying up bundles of grain," Joseph said. "When we were finished, your bundles made a circle around mine, and they all bowed down to it!"

Joseph's brothers grew even angrier with him.

"He thinks that we should all bow down to him!" they said.

Color in Joseph and his brothers.

 Find the stickers to finish the picture.

How many brothers does Joseph have? ☐

How many bundles of grain are bowing down? ☐

 Can you find eleven names hidden in this grid?

Simeon   Judah   Reuben   Issachar
Gad   Dan   Asher   Levi   Benjamin
Zebulun   Naphtali

S	Z	A	W	C	G	F	V	T	G	B
A	B	E	N	J	A	M	I	N	D	A
R	Z	E	N	U	D	B	V	E	N	S
Z	E	B	A	S	I	M	E	O	N	S
I	B	M	P	S	E	O	L	N	B	E
R	U	E	H	N	H	J	Z	M	I	L
E	L	V	T	Z	L	E	V	R	J	B
U	U	D	A	N	S	A	R	H	U	U
B	N	X	L	B	N	M	J	F	D	E
E	W	U	I	S	S	A	C	H	A	R
N	J	O	L	A	V	F	C	N	H	D

Joseph's brothers had had enough of him.

"Let's take his coat and kill him," said the brothers. But Reuben said, "No, let's throw him in the well and leave him there."

 Find the stickers to finish the picture.

Later, some merchants passed by on their way to Egypt.

"Now we can get rid of Joseph!" Judah said. "We can sell him to the merchants as a slave."

The merchants bought Joseph for twenty pieces of silver.

The brothers decided to tell their father that a wild animal had killed Joseph. So they put goat's blood on Joseph's coat.

Find the stickers to finish the picture.
Find the bag with twenty pieces of silver.
Follow the lines to find which merchant it belongs to.

JOSEPH IN PRISON

In Egypt, Joseph's master was a man called Potiphar.

    Joseph worked hard for Potiphar, but Potiphar thought his wife was falling in love with Joseph, so he had him put in prison.

 Can you spot five differences between these two pictures?

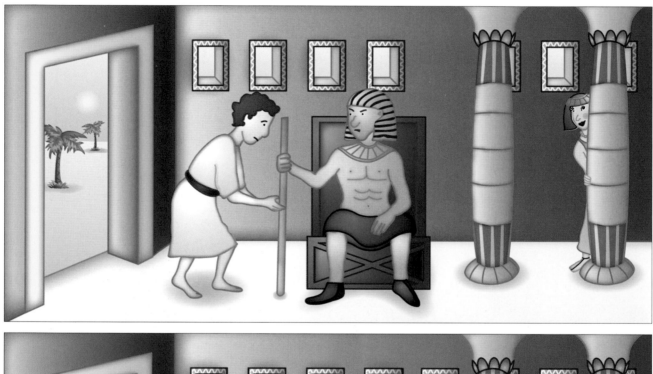

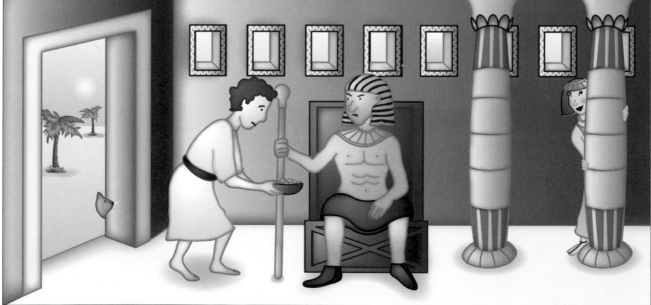

One of the other prisoners was the butler of Pharaoh, the Egyptian King. One day, he told Joseph, "I had a strange dream last night. Can you tell me what it means?"

"God will tell us both," said Joseph. "What did you dream?"

"I dreamt I had a vine with three branches," said the butler, "and I made wine for Pharaoh."

"It means that in three days Pharaoh will set you free," Joseph told him.

Three days later, just as Joseph had said, Pharaoh set his butler free. The butler was amazed, and he told Pharaoh about Joseph.

 Find the stickers to finish the picture.
How many sets of three can you find in the picture?

Some time later, Pharaoh had a dream that puzzled him. He remembered what his butler had told him about Joseph, and he asked for him to be brought from prison.

"I dreamed that I saw seven skinny cows eat seven fat cows," said Pharaoh. "Can you tell me what the dream means?"

"God can tell us both," said Joseph. "The dream means that Egypt will have seven years of plenty. But then there will be seven years of famine, when there will be very little food."

 Find the stickers to finish the picture.

139

Pharaoh put Joseph in charge of Egypt's food stores. During seven years of plenty, Joseph saved the extra food. Then there was famine, but there was plenty of food for everyone in Egypt.

Back in Canaan, Joseph's family didn't have enough to eat. His brothers came to Egypt to buy grain. They didn't know that the person in charge was Joseph. But he recognized them.

He decided to test his brothers to see if they had changed. He filled all his brothers' sacks with grain. When no one was looking, he hid a silver cup in Benjamin's sack.

Find the stickers to finish the picture.

Find the stickers to finish the picture.
Which trail leads to Benjamin's sack?

a
b
c
d
e

When the cup was found in Benjamin's sack, the brothers were arrested and brought before Joseph.

Joseph said that the brothers could go home—except for Benjamin. Judah begged Joseph to let Benjamin go, too.

"We have already caused our father, Jacob, to lose one son," he said. "If he loses Benjamin too, he will die of sorrow."

Joseph saw that his brothers were sorry.

"I am your brother Joseph!" he cried. "Bring Father to Egypt, and we will be together again." So Jacob was reunited with his lost son, and the family lived together again.

 Find the story stickers and put them in the right order. Read the scrolls to help you.

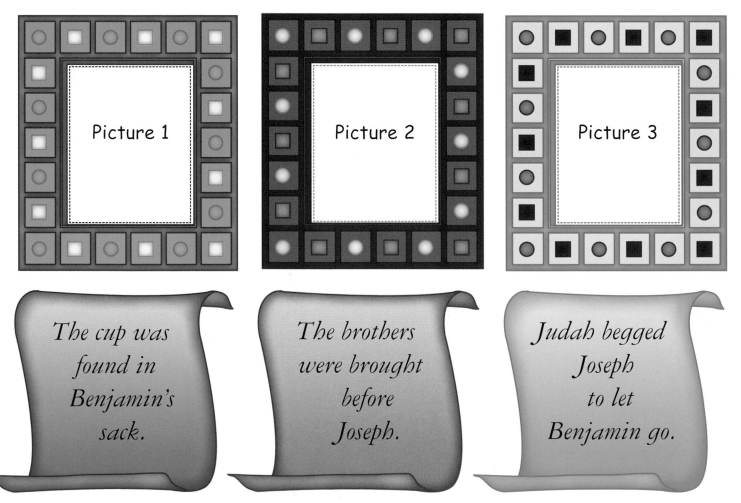

| Picture 1 | Picture 2 | Picture 3 |

The cup was found in Benjamin's sack.

The brothers were brought before Joseph.

Judah begged Joseph to let Benjamin go.

Color in the picture of Joseph and Jacob's happy reunion.
Can you find five mice hidden in the picture?

Can you spot five differences between these two pictures of Joseph?

Page 130

Page 131

Page 133

Pages 134/135

Page 137

Pages 138/139

Pages 140/141

Page 142

COPY THE PICTURE

Jacob was an old man who had twelve sons.

 Copy this picture of Jacob, square by square, then color it in.

SPOT THE DIFFERENCE

Jacob loved all his sons, but Joseph, the youngest, was his favorite.

 One of these pictures is slightly different from the rest. Can you spot it?

a

b

c

d

e

f

DOT TO DOT

The other brothers were very jealous when Jacob gave Jospeh a beautiful, colorful coat.

Join the dots to finish the picture. Now color it in.

WHAT DOESN'T BELONG?

One day, Joseph told his brothers about a strange dream he had.
"I dreamed your bundles of grain bowed down to mine," he said.

Can you spot five things in the
picture that don't belong?

149

FINISH THE PICTURE

The brothers thought that Joseph was a show-off, and wanted to get rid of him.

Can you draw the stripes on Joseph's coat?

JUST COLORING

They decided to take Joseph's coat, and throw him in an old well.

 Color in this picture of the brothers throwing Joseph in the well.

DOT TO DOT

Just then, some merchants selling camels passed by, on their way to Egypt.

Join the dots to finish the picture. Now color it in.

MATCHING GAME

The brothers sold Joseph to the merchants for twenty pieces of silver.
The merchants sold him as a slave in Egypt.

 Can you find the shadow which exactly matches this picture?

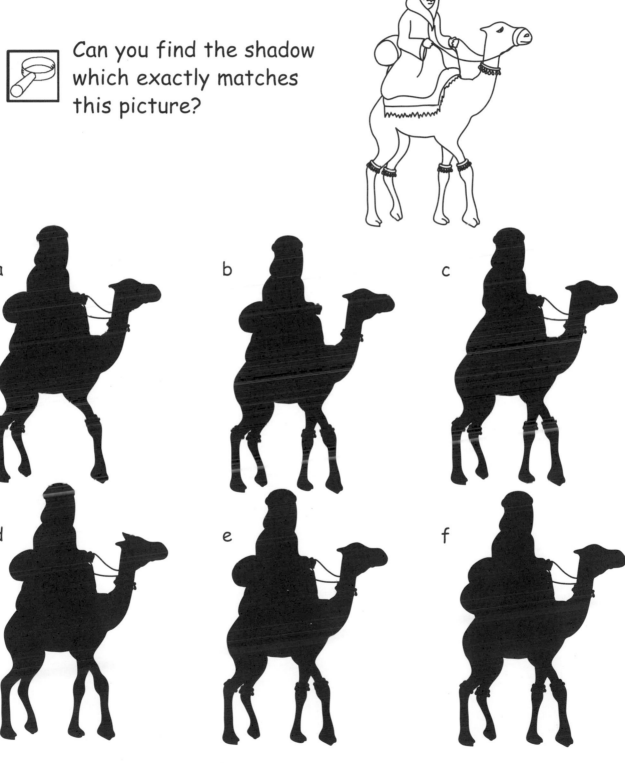

a

b

c

d

e

f

AMAZING MAZE

In Egpyt, Joseph became very good at understanding people's dreams.
One day, he was even taken to talk to the Pharaoh about his dream.

Can you help Joseph and the guard find their way through the palace to meet the Pharaoh?

FIND TWO THE SAME

In his dream, the Pharaoh saw seven thin cows eat seven fat cows.

Look closely at these seven cows. Only two of them are exactly the same. Can you spot them?

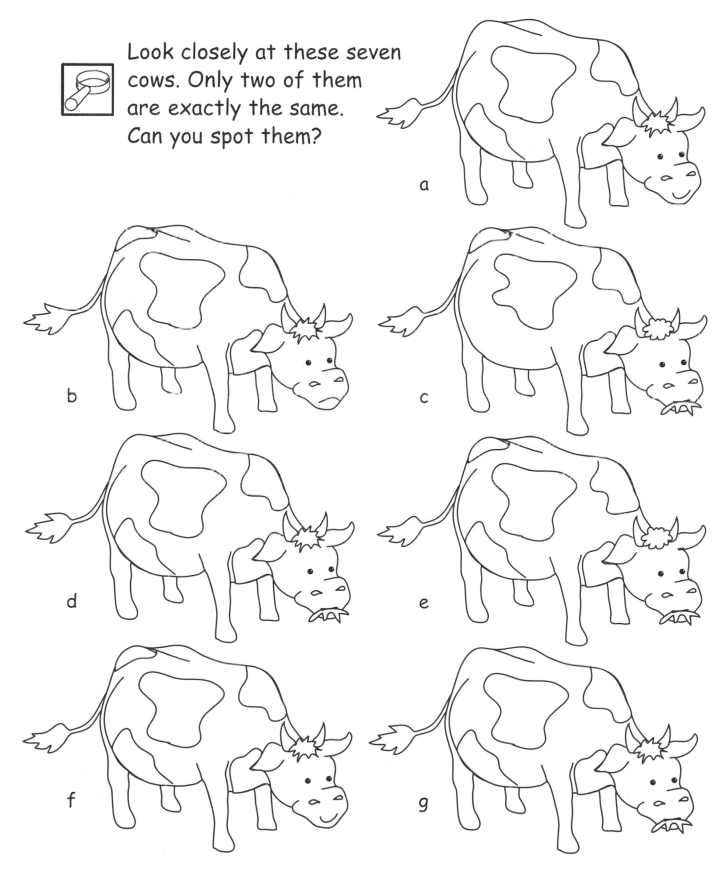

155

FINISH THE PICTURE

Joseph explained the Pharoah's dream. There would be seven years of good harvests, followed by seven years of bad harvests.

 Can you make these four pictures of the Pharaoh look exactly the same?

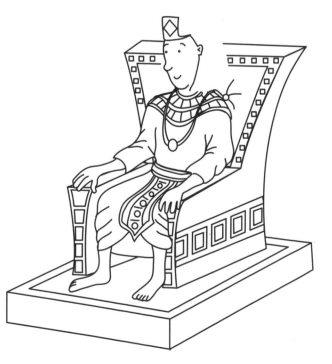 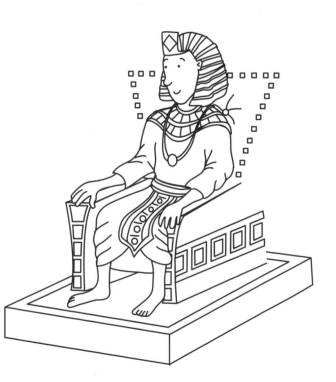

WORDSEARCH

The Pharaoh put Joseph in charge of Egypt's food stores. Joseph saved food for when the bad harvests came.

Can you find these words in the grid?

CAMEL   JOSEPH
GRAIN   EGYPT
CANAAN   BAG
JACOB   DREAM
MERCHANT   FAMINE

Y	E	C	B	D	U	I	R	Q
H	N	O	O	P	L	M	C	T
I	I	E	C	A	N	A	A	N
V	M	G	A	M	H	E	M	A
N	A	Y	J	K	P	R	E	H
I	F	P	Z	Q	E	D	L	C
A	G	T	A	E	S	D	Z	R
R	X	A	A	W	O	E	O	E
G	Y	B	B	T	J	R	P	M

CROSSWORD

Joseph's brothers were starving, so they went to Egypt to ask for some food. They did not recognise Joseph when they saw him.

Fill in the crossword using the pictures as clues. Some letters have been added to help you.

1 down

2 across

3 across

4 down

5 down

6 across

EYE SPY

Joseph decided to test his brothers. He hid a silver cup in Benjamin's sack, then had him arrested for stealing. When the others begged Joseph to let Benjamin go, Joseph knew they had changed.

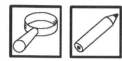 Can you find the silver cup?
Now color in the picture.

COMPLETE THE SCENE

Jospeh's father, Jacob, was brought to Egypt, and the whole family was reunited!

 Joseph and his family are having a celebration feast. Can you draw in the food?

The Birth of Jesus

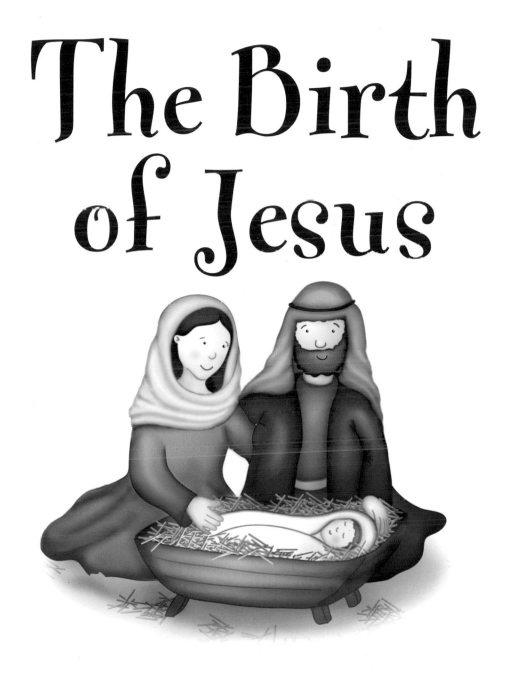

The Birth of Jesus answers are on page 214-215

AN ANGEL APPEARS

Once there was a carpenter named Joseph, who lived in a town called Nazareth. He was married to a woman named Mary.

One day, Mary got a very special message from God. The angel Gabriel appeared before her and said, "God has blessed you, Mary. You will have a baby, and you will name him Jesus. He will be the son of God, whose kingdom will last forever."

 Find the stickers to complete the picture of Joseph in his workshop.

Join the dots to finish the picture, then color it in.

GOING TO BETHLEHEM

A few months later, the emperor in Rome sent out an order. There was to be a census. This meant that everyone had to go back to the town where they were born to be counted.

Joseph had to go back to Bethlehem, and Mary went with him. She was going to have her baby soon, so she rode on a donkey.

The journey was very long, but at last they reached Bethlehem.

 Help Mary and Joseph find their way from Nazareth to Bethlehem.
Find the stickers to decorate the path.

Bethlehem

165

NO ROOM AT THE INN

It was very late when Mary and Joseph arrived in Bethlehem. They tried to find an inn for the night, but everywhere they asked there was no room at the inn.

 All the inns in Bethlehem were full because of the census. Can you spot five differences between these two pictures of Mary and Joseph looking for an inn?

There was only one inn left in Bethlehem for them to try. At first the innkeeper said, "I'm sorry. All the rooms are full." But he felt sorry for Mary, so he added, "You can sleep in my stable. I will put down some fresh straw for you to sleep on. Your little donkey can stay there too."

Can you join the dots to make the stable?
Now put the stickers in the picture and color it in.

THE BABY IS BORN

That night Mary's baby was born.
Mary wrapped him in soft cloths to keep him warm
and snug. There was no cradle, so she laid him in the manger.
"We will call the baby Jesus," she said, "just as the angel said."

Find the sticker of baby Jesus, and put him in the manger.
All the animals in the scene have babies too. Can you find
the right stickers to go with each grown-up animal?

GOOD NEWS!

In the fields outside Bethlehem, shepherds were watching their flocks. Suddenly light filled the sky, and angels appeared.

"Do not be frightened," the angels said. "We bring good news. A baby has been born in Bethlehem, and he will bring joy to the whole world. Glory to God and peace on earth!"

The shepherds were very excited. They rushed to Bethlehem to find the wonderful baby.

Three of these angels are the same, but one is different. Can you spot the difference? Now find the stickers to finish the scene.

171

A BRIGHT NEW STAR

In a land far away in the East, there were three wise men who watched the sky every night. One night a new star appeared, bigger and brighter than all the others. The wise men knew that it meant a new king had been born.

"We must follow the star," they said, "and find the king!"

They traveled over mountains and across deserts, following the star shining brightly above them.

Help the wise men decide which path to take to get to Baby Jesus.

a

b

c

THE WISE MEN'S GIFTS

The star led the three wise men all the way to Bethlehem. There they found Baby Jesus in the stable, with Mary and Joseph.

The wise men gave Baby Jesus the gifts they had brought.

"I have brought gold," said the first wise man.

"I have brought frankincense," said the second.

"I have brought myrrh," said the third.

They were gifts for a special baby, who was God's gift to the world.

 The wise men should be holding their presents for Baby Jesus, but the presents are missing! Find the sticker that fits each space.

Now use the code below to color the whole scene.

Can you spot six differences between these two pictures of Mary and Joseph with Baby Jesus?

Page 162

Pages 164/165

Page 167

Nazareth

Pages 168/169

Pages 170/171

Pages 172/173

Page 174

EYE SPY

Joseph, a carpenter, was married to a young woman called Mary.

 Joseph has lost some of his tools. Can you find these five tools in the picture?

MATCHING GAME

An angel told Mary that she would have a baby, who would be the Son of God.

Can you match this angel with the right shadow?

a

b

c

d

e

DOT TO DOT

Just before her baby was born, Mary and Joseph had to go to Bethlehem to be counted for a census. It was a long journey, so Mary rode on a donkey.

 Join the dots to finish the picture. Now color it in.

SPOT THE DIFFERENCE

An innkeeper let them stay in his stable, because all the rooms were full.

Which picture of the innkeeper is different?

a

b

c

d

e

f

HOW MANY?

It was cosy and warm in the stable.

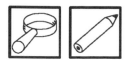 How many animals beginning with the letter C can you find in the picture? Now color it in.

WHERE'S MY MOMMY?

Mary and Joseph had to share the stable with lots of animals.

Draw a line between each baby animal and its mommy.

COPY THE PICTURE

When Mary's very special baby, Jesus, was born, she wrapped him in warm cloths and laid him in the manger to sleep.

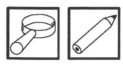 Copy this picture of Baby Jesus in the manger, square by square, then color it in.

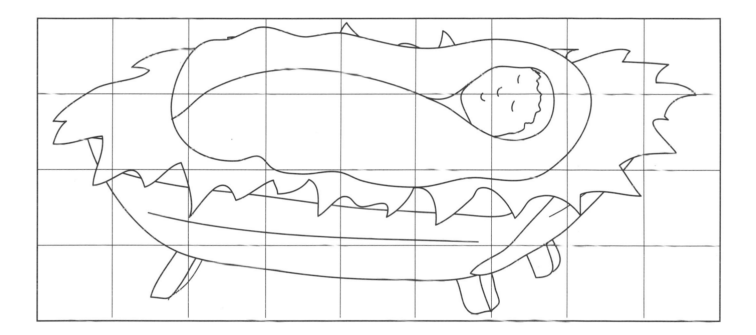

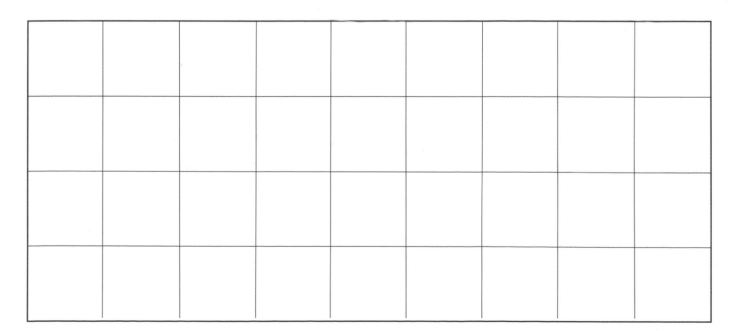

MYSTERY PICTURE

A star shone brightly in the sky that night, to tell the world
a king had been born.

Carefully shade the dotted areas to reveal the hidden picture.

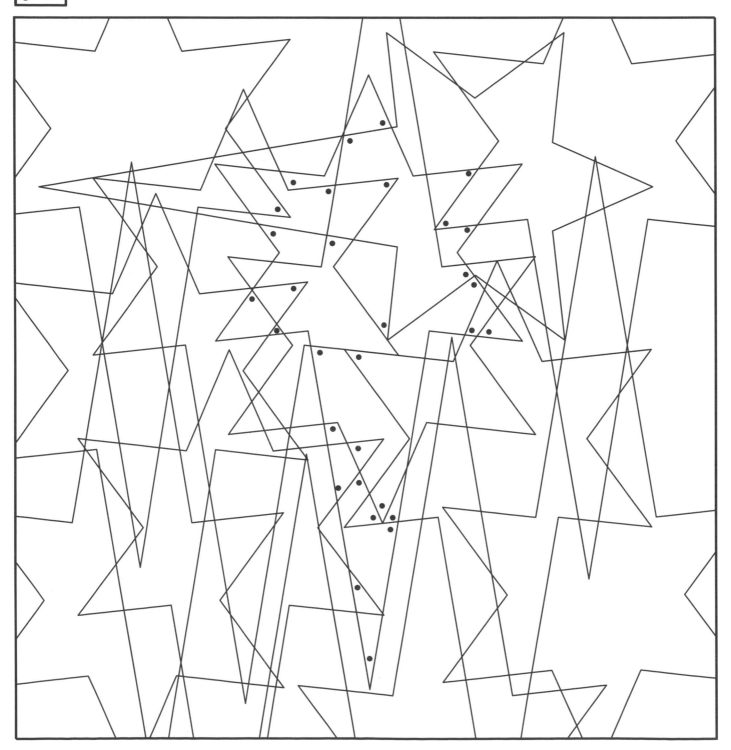

FINISH THE PICTURES

A choir of angels told the shepherds on the hillside that Baby Jesus had been born.

Can you make these four pictures of a shepherd look the same?

The shepherds found Baby Jesus in a stable, just as the angels had said.

 These five things are all hidden in the picture. How many of them can you spot? Now color in the picture.

DOT TO DOT

Even the animals joined in, worshipping Baby Jesus.

Join the dots to see which animal is looking at Baby Jesus. Now color in the picture.

FOLLOW THE STRINGS

In a faraway land, three wise men saw the star, and knew that a king had been born. They set out with gifts to find the baby.

Follow the strings to help each wise man find the right gift.

MATCHING SHADOWS

The wise men traveled by night, following the star in the night sky.

Draw a line between each shadow, and the person it matches.

CROSSWORD

The star led the wise men to Bethlehem, where they found Jesus.

Fill in the crossword using the pictures as clues. Some letters have been added to help you.

5 down

2 down

3 down

4 M G

P

4 across

5

6 S T L

1 down

6 across

WORDSEARCH

The wise men gave Jesus gifts of gold, frankincense and myrrh.

Can you find these words in the grid?

DONKEY   JOSEPH
PEACE   MARY
GIFTS   GOLD
SHEEP   MYRRH
JESUS   INNKEEPER

I	N	N	K	E	E	P	E	R
S	J	K	D	O	N	K	E	Y
H	E	O	G	O	L	T	N	L
E	S	M	S	P	N	P	M	O
E	U	Y	P	E	E	E	Y	L
V	S	R	P	A	P	E	Y	D
M	A	R	Y	C	R	H	R	L
C	A	H	B	E	P	S	O	O
C	G	O	L	S	T	F	I	G

JUST COLORING

A very special baby had been born, who was God's gift to the world.

Color in the picture.

Daniel in the Lions' Den

Daniel in the Lions' Den answers are on page 216

DOT TO DOT

Daniel was a good man who loved God, and prayed every day. He was also King Darius' most trusted advisor and friend.

Join the dots to finish the picture. Now color it in.

194

SPOT THE DIFFERENCE

Whenever he had a problem, King Darius always wanted to know what Daniel thought about it.

 These pictures of Darius all look the same, but one is slightly different. Can you spot it?

a

b

c

d

WHAT DOESN'T BELONG?

King Darius' other advisors were jealous of Daniel. They talked behind his back, until they came up with a plan to get rid of him.

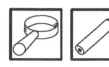 Can you find five modern things that don't belong in this picture? Now colour it in.

MATCHING GAME

They tricked King Darius into making a new law. Everyone must pray only to the King, or be thrown to the lions!

Can you draw a line between this picture and its shadow?

a

b

c

d

e

AMAZING MAZE

Daniel's enemies waited until Daniel knelt down to pray to God.
Then they sent soldiers to arrest him.

Which path should the guards take to arrest Daniel?

EYE SPY

King Darius and Daniel knew that they had been tricked, but Daniel had broken the new law. He had to be thrown to the lions!

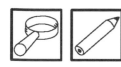 How many things beginning with the letter D can you find in the picture? Now color it in.

199

DOT TO DOT

Daniel was thrown in a den full of hungry lions, and a stone was rolled over the top to seal it.

Join the dots to finish the picture. Now colour it in.

JUST COLORING

Daniel was not afraid. He just knelt down and prayed for God to keep him safe. God knew that Daniel had done nothing wrong, so he sent an angel to close the lions' mouths.

Color in this picture.

WORDSEARCH

In the morning King Darius rushed to the lions' den, to find out what had happened to his friend, Daniel.

Can you find these words in the grid?

DANIEL
LIONS
DARIUS
PALACE
LAW

PRAYER
ADVISOR
ANGEL
DEN
KING

E	M	W	P	A	N	G	E	L
C	H	A	P	E	E	O	I	E
A	E	L	S	R	Y	D	Y	I
L	D	Q	N	X	A	V	R	N
A	J	V	O	R	W	Y	S	A
P	K	L	I	Y	P	K	E	D
C	V	U	L	S	J	O	E	R
S	S	A	Q	W	O	N	I	H
K	I	N	G	C	V	R	B	L

JUST COLORING

When the stone was rolled back, everyone was amazed. Daniel was safe and sound. "Your God is great!" cried Darius. "Everyone should pray to him!"

 Color in the picture.

Answers—David and Goliath

Pages 98/99

There are 15 sheep.

Pages 102/103

Page 104

Page 106

Page 108

Page 109

Picture 1   Picture 2

Picture 3   Picture 4

Page 112

Pages 114

It is a picture of a harp.

Pages 115

Picture b is different.

Page 116
Path c leads to David's sling.

Page 117
David is chasing away a bear.

Page 118
Soldiers d and f are the same.

Page 119
David has the slingshot.

His brother has the shield.

The Philistine soldier has the sword.

Page 121

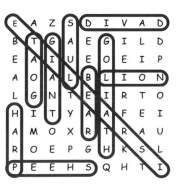

Page 122
Shadow c exactly matches the picture of David.

Page 123

Page 124
Did you spot a shield, a sword, the sun, sheep, a spike, sandals, a slingshot, and stones?

Page 125
There are 10 swords in the big picture.

Page 126

Page 127

Page 133

Page 135

Sack c contains
twenty pieces of silver.
It belongs to merchant c.

Page 136

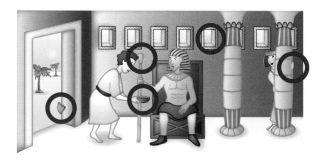

Page 137

There are 7 sets of 3: 3 dream
stickers, 3 bars on window,
3 seats, 3 bowls, 3 spoons,
3 prisoners (including Joseph) and
3 branches on the vine.

Pages 138/139

There are 7 fans, 7 cats, 7 pots,
7 fat cows and 7 skinny cows.

Page 141

Sack d belongs
to Benjamin.

Page 142

Picture 1   Picture 2   Picture 3

Page 143

Page 144

Page 146

Picture d is different.

Page 147

Page 148/149

Page 152

Page 153
The right shadow for the picture is e.

Page 154

Page 155
Cows d and g are exactly the same.

Page 157

Page 158

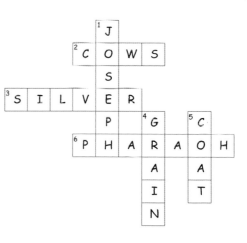

Page 159

Page 163

Pages 164/165

Page 166

Pages 167

Page 170/171

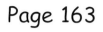

Pages 172/173

The wise men must follow path c.

Pages 176

Page 177

Page 178

Shadow c is the right one for the angel.

Page 179

Page 180

Picture e is different.

Page 181

Did you spot a cow, calf, chicken, chick, and cat?

Page 182

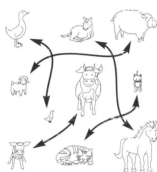

Page 184

It is a picture of the star.

Page 186

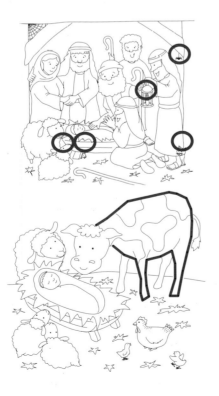

Page 187

Page 188

Wise man 1 goes with present b.

Wise man 2 goes with present a.

Wise man 3 goes with present c.

Page 189

Page 190

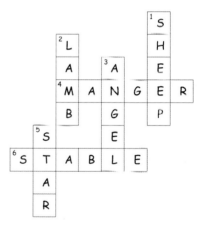

Page 191

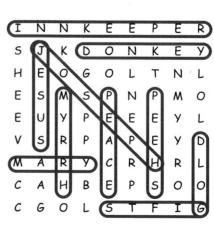

Answers—Daniel in the Lions' Den

Page 194

Page 195

Picture b is different.

Page 196

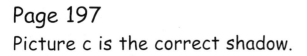

Page 197

Picture c is the correct shadow.

Page 198

Page 199

Did you spot the donkey, den, dog, Darius, and Daniel?

Page 200

Page 202

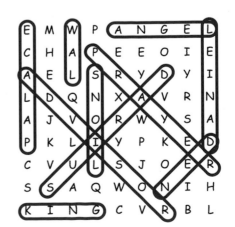